I Always Carry My Bones

Winner of the Iowa Poetry Prize

I Always Carry My Bones

poems by Felicia Zamora

University of Iowa Press | Iowa City

University of Iowa Press, Iowa City 52242
Copyright © 2021 by Felicia Zamora
uipress.uiowa.edu
Printed in the United States of America
Design by Sara T. Sauers
Cover art, *Lago en el Cielo*, by Silvia Andrade. www.silviaandrade.com
Printed on acid-free paper

Library of Congress Cataloging-in-Publication Data
Names: Zamora, Felicia M., author.
Title: I Always Carry My Bones / Felicia Zamora.
Description: Iowa City: University of Iowa Press, [2021] |
Series: Iowa Poetry Prize |
Identifiers: LCCN 2020039764 (print) |
LCCN 2020039765 (ebook) |
ISBN 9781609387761 (paperback; acid-free paper) |
ISBN 9781609387778 (ebook)
Subjects: LCGFT: Poetry.
Classification: LCC PS3626.A6278 I18 2021 (print) |
LCC PS3626.A6278 (ebook) | DDC 811/.6—dc23
LC record available at https://lccn.loc.gov/2020039764
LC ebook record available at https://lccn.loc.gov/2020039765

for Diana & TC

Show me how ruin makes a home / out of hip bones.

—OCEAN VUONG
Night Sky with Exit Wounds

You don't seem too haunted, but you haunted.

—TERRANCE HAYES
American Sonnets for My Past and Future Assassin

we say our own names when we pray.

—DANEZ SMITH
Don't Call Us Dead

Contents

Where the Carriage of My Cells Catch

I Always Carry My Bones

In Breach of Etiquette

Homing Anatomy

Your body finds its way to water
by instinct; a cellular thoughtfulness:
a trillion converters of energy, in hunt,
bound together in make of you, O
organism, unknown to quiet; how hum
of you influences space, adds to exquisite
cacophony in resound. No solitude lives
in these tendrils of lough, not unlike
the body—press an ear to rib cage
& chatter consumes listener; so much wet
resides here—you feel your cells crowd
surfaces of flesh, flush outward to attract
the clouds & damp & hollow close, closer
still to all your teeming; you organ
of encounter: heart of reeds, lung
of dew, stomach of grasses; what dwells
in land, dwells in you; throat of tide, river
in your limbic system, brain harbinger
of wing flaps & cattle moans, of sky's breath
to tremor all branches; the world in quaver
depends on perspective, tip or trunk. See
your roots burrow from cranium to sternum
to distal phalange; again you go with hunting
an inner seeking, you colony of cells. How wind
touches the surface of lake, a hard hush; you
witness a stream just beneath underbelly, in forge
of its own path, despite—what flows
orbicular, finds new methods of sprawl.

Bodies & Water

I think about my kneecaps, my ear canal, the slight webbing between toes & fingers; I think about brown bodies, my body; how my belly ebbs & sinks & floats & calms in water; I think about black bodies, about statistics, how 65% of black American children cannot swim; 60 for Latinx children; 79 from low-income families. How statistics hold history in the sharp end of a tack; my brother & me thrown out of swim lessons for *causing trouble*; limbs reach & tread, lacking *know-how*; how a statistic takes a term like *access*, wads it into a crumpled shape, in search of any receptacle other than a docket; our cells contain wet & wombing history of sea & salt in our nervous systems; our cells crave water & in turn crave equity; no magic equation exists to explain why what's *made* of water *wants* water; no need. The human body consists of organs & tissues & hydrogen & calcium & sodium & chlorine & water & water & water & water. Why must my water offend your water? Fuck your count of my offensive features—labia, mustache, mammary glands, black hair on my nipples, thoughts in my cranium, uterus, hopes sewn in cerebrum, words readied at tongue— you dominate narrative: a scratched record caught in dilapidated loop, white noise that coats ammonia down my throat to attempt erasure; history of *attempts*. You cannot remove water from water, sea from sea.

Devil's Tongue

Born of heat. Born from the world's belly,
endemic to home— México, peduncle
of me & yet, I cross lines toed in dirt,
lines drawn in thought that any species
may be contained if enclosed hard enough,
long enough, if watched & guarded.
Speak me— no, not *Ferocactus latispinus*, not

my Latin name, not my colonized name—
speak me from crown to neck to vascular tissues;
speak me from spines. See my claws
& be warned. Speak me out of the mouths
of serpents. How Quetzalcoatl despised
subjugation, adopted the human condition,
& my body a shrine to terrestrial

connectivity. Who I am: one who flowers
late in autumn, late in winter, spitting fire
from my areoles, my sunken spots, places
where my spine rises & rises. Call me,
shallow root. How my systems drag wide
close to surfaces so I may imbibe what I need
before evaporation. Volume of me, expands

when I must hold; contracts, when I must go
without. To those who wish to poke holes in me,
keep me caged by gates, withhold resources
from me to let me dry up: hear my whispers
in tepid sand—*biomimicry*—how I adapt away
from you—*biomimicry*—as if to chant my way
into something worthy of your affection.

Closer

My chin to the ardent sky. How you never told me about the whiteness of sunlight. How sunlight contains all colors; all colors mixed up & in collection, appear white. How this light heavies my eyelids, here in nape of this rock formation, this snaking trail in the valley of a valley, desert tongue germinates inside these jaws. How I imagine your hands in weight upon my shoulders, wrists, ankles, jugular, drawing blood because you, too, contain the spikes & spines & lineage of cacti: short growing season, long dormancy; one may even think you a ghost, illusion of a wanting mind, if these ocular cavities didn't resemble a blurred & sepia photograph, first studied & inhaled mothballs & cedar chests at the age of sixteen. A photograph in mirror of my ridge of cheeks, slope of nose, square of my mandible in hold of my infant body tight to your chest; still a clutch in incubation in your arms. How you never told me this light passes, tangles in the atmosphere & scatters. Smog & dust & particles reconfigure & the blue, the blue in the light separates most. The blue hangs the sky, reminds us of pieces & wholes & untetherings. You never told me. How could you? You coyote, voiceless among the ridge, miles out from me, in spook if I draw one step closer. You whose face floats amid the mulberries at twilight, as the firefly abdomens illuminate, then darken, illuminate, then darken, illuminate, then darken.

Memory of Sheep Rustling

We had renters. Summer at the motel brought wheels to gravel—sounds &—car doors on rusty hinges, cowboy boots on concrete, flirtations of language, English & Spanish, outlines of strangers absorbed into the heft of humidity; 1984; July; how heat & wet-corn inhaled mixed the senses of time, of space in my six-year-old brain. On tiptoes, my nose on knuckles barely rested over the counter's lip; mulberry-stained fingers. I watched him do business. His semitruck voice boomed, *$29*; the nightly room rate; the man in the cowboy hat shifted his weight over flies & erratic ticks of the office's oscillating fan; he inspected the two-foot Christmas tree adorned in webs mantled on the chartreuse refrigerator; a poster hung on the wall, $30 crossed out to $28, ~~$28~~ to $25, ~~$25~~ to $23; he had a rate for everyone. The man dug a wallet from his pocket; his hands calloused; his eyes dark—like mine; his hair black—like mine; *Veintiuno?* & he showed bills to my grandfather. The 5:30 sun sliced through the blinds, casting an uneven strip across my grandfather's mouth; noir in all senses, *Git!* he pushed weight of his hand on my back toward the screen door. I hunched on the step & watched two girls run alongside the sheep pasture just west of the motel; a boy heaved duffle bags out of a truck bed, *¿Te quedas aquí también?* & grinned at me. After wheels hit gravel again & bedding needed to be washed & wounds tended where the lasso tore my flesh, he ate peas & liver from his tv tray, barely a glance, *You stupid little spic. You want the wholegoddamntown to know you're as dirty as them?* On the screen, a woman touched her toes in pink spandex suspenders. Air in my lungs grew dense; wrecking ball of gut; prickles engulfed all inches & I understood injury & epithet & cage & the neck of a sheep yanked in rope. I swung open the screen door & ran deep to pasture where earth & wool stung my chest, where my bleat echoed & howled to the deciduous dusk: *them them them them them them me me me me me me.*

Dear Coyote

How the bathwater mildews the lip of the tub, cold to any touch of toe, faucet leaks still; how calcium builds on metal in thick layers: here beneath the lamella of lime & rust, a body chips out. At first, the knuckle bones, a fist without flesh stretches to the plaster sky. Next, the spinal column in only the cervical & sacral vertebrae—to bend fingers to feel weight of bowel & bladder, as in a child who urinates the bed until seven because she believes you return in shadows—with the cervical, a tether to the thin skeletal muscle. To speak *diaphragm*, a contraction & flatten behind walls of flesh during inhale: a vacuum at the base of chest; vacuum in which to suffocate, suffocate over sinks, next to public restroom toilets, on playgrounds where blonde kids create her history with their saliva on her cheeks, upon inaugural bleach of her mustache she doesn't know yet about you, dear coyote, about your clever mind, jaw of fangs in rip of instinct, need; the migration in your belly, her belly.

For Survival of Migration:
Or That Which They Cannot Devour

Let's say your body's a caterpillar, an accordion in scooch
among branches. Let's say you crave; yes, you crave
the latex & cardiac glycosides; how you really crave carnage—
the deconstruction of systems—bite & suck between mandibles
& in the damage of cells, the milky toxin exudes, & you being
metamorphosis minded, believe in the announcement of names,
guts of you pull, pull toward the known unknown. When voice
resonates in you, you in whispers atop your dorsal wing surface
milkweed, milkweed, milkweed finds the tongueless tonguing
five petals, fused stamen filaments encircling a five-
membrane corona. O hair, O hood, O inner horn. How
you long for each—to imbibe poison, you become poison.
What you carry in crawl to pupa in your belly. Crawl of natural
defense. You wrap in your own bonnet, taper at abdomen, a pendant
of golden specks, a belt of earthly stars in ornament. Let's say
you rest & transformation hollows, renders both form & ability,
then wake to wingspans & flight buried in your exoskeleton,
toxicity of milkweed—for those who imagine you in their esophagus:
the effects of toxins in limbs, in brain; to those who find you delectable,
exotic, cageable, containable: the sores of poison. Your migration:
to protect our story; an evolution to that which they cannot devour.

Motel

We don't talk about
the fleas, the cat
named *Baby* on a leash
inside, the mice
or Baby's longing for mice,
the switch to light the motel sign
we couldn't touch, the washer
we couldn't touch, the lawnmower
we couldn't touch, *you're not*
smart enough to work this, the tv
remote we couldn't touch, 1966
Dodge Charger in metallic cobalt
on blocks inside the carport
with the collapsed roof
we couldn't touch, the empty
room up the stairs—
first on the left—our uncle's
seventies weights & collared shirts
we couldn't touch, grandma's fake
pearls, color of her skin, her Sunday
pearls she kept on the nightstand
we couldn't touch, the old shower
jimmy-rigged to work as a sink
& how we used a hose
to rinse a plate, the crack
of office window where my head
shattered, the sound
of glass falling in the ear, years

to fix, the lack of fix
in any vocabulary, the toilet
revving like a rocket ship
in the bathroom of seafoam-green
tile & mildew & razor blade
between forefinger & thumb
for one more *go home wetback,*
the orange shag carpet
that made our bare feet squirm,
the living room below the stairs
we couldn't enter, the story
of the pool table we couldn't
touch a thing of power, the diner
closed & made into a living room
& bedroom & kitchen & bathroom
for four, specifically three
brown kids *who won't amount*
to anything, the smell of must & lye
of his unwashed body, his leg whittled
to bone from atrophy, what sharing
a bed with my mother
until I was eleven means
to me now, how empty space
belonged to *junk* rather than
three children growing, how we all
grow *out* of something, how difficult
it is to say *us, me, we,* & really I mean
Mel, Felicia, Joe, the never-birthday

parties & thinking I had done
something wrong to never
warrant celebration, smell
of pilot light in winter jaw chatter,
smell of her hair when we kissed
her goodnight with the sun pedestalled
above the tree line, her knuckles
cracked & bloody & how we knew
what salve did but not why
she wouldn't, the gravel parking lot
& how it expanded out into a sea
of town & sneers & corn &
steeples & whispers & fists &
faith & grit & stone of when
a human heart must, the hinges
on a screen door—slightly rusted
as a mantra—closing at my back
from a distance too far to measure,
too heavy to look back.

Labels & Cadavers & Superimposed Fathers

Her stomach & spleen sit comfortably right,
not the anatomically correct left; her lung holds
only two lobes to my three, your three. You see,
her body a mirror of symmetry inside & outside
our brains. They call her organs *backwards*, call her
organs *mutations*, label her body *flipflop innards*
& my chest heaves & spasms at how labels & finger-
pointing & jaw-punching contort a body & mind
of a little girl the age of seven. Yet she's on a slab
at 99 defying them all, CNN says. Her body a mystery
until she reveals herself in rigor mortis. Her body
a donation to science & science another altar
of our failed religions. Her body makes me think
of brown bodies, of black bodies, of queer bodies
who receive words of slander, of othering over &
over at our eardrums, to our faces in relentless cycle.
Words carve in me, slash at me, twist me O
bramble tumulus in containment of me. Science, I
often love you, yet, in your inceptions, you weave
broken labels & constructs—let us consider *race*—
how you allow a human mind to corrupt you
& little brown girls bleed from the flounder.
No genetic evidence exists to separate my bone
from ancestors' bones, from bones of any human
bone of bone of bone. You let Morton collect skulls.
You let him scavenge catacombs, stuff skulls
with pepper seeds, later led shot—for braincase.
Braincase of what? Father of scientific
racism. A hierarchy of craniometry

lives in my wounds, the wounds of bodies made
inferior with labels, with actions behind labels.
I ask the owners of words that claw, that gnaw,
that sting, to take them back. Hold the weight
of your own words; hold them in your throat—
how the penitent tongue soils the communion wafer
with viscous saliva, how the body of any savior
allows you to feast as its father, its host—
& call into question your own hunger; swallow
the rigidity of language. Chew words in your jaws
until your molars grind down to dust. Consider
your speech tastes sour to the tongue, aortic
valve, temporal lobe—how our organs in skeletal
structures connect us, beyond your labels, in genes
we all share the same collections, beyond cadavers
you wish of us—your superimposed fathers leave us
to reassemble our anatomies & voices in your mouths.

Dear Coyote

I stitch the stars in patterns of your chin, your kneecap, your rib, your gait: a constellation of absence. I map your body, a celestial cartography to understand my own echo, my own cave in the torso, cave of undoing. When you beat my brother's face with a sack of potatoes, when he bruised & you drew the burlap back for blood, did you smell lilac, believe your fists made us into something beautiful? When you opened our mother with knuckles scented with other vaginas, did you believe in your gift, passed? I cup my breasts in the mirror & consider the tissues of violence; if I crack my neck, cleave at the thyroid & pull out the medulla oblongata, will I cross-section the parts of you that continue to wound? I am a poor butcher & an even poorer butcher's daughter. My fingers fail to sew you into being for each star a sun, in bleed of light, destructive & vitalizing. We both know this thread & needle ignite in each baste, each backstitch of form. We both hold the weight of ash in our lungs.

Any Stretch of Imagination

How the raven embodies wings, a gait meant to scatter firmament, undo patterns of jet streams & beams of light—yet, it cannot escape the fire of bullets in the air, bullets from our mouths, bullets in load of an H&K P2000 (*double action*, they say as a seeking of impression, a seeking seeded in arteries in fill with lead & casings) in press of sky in press of a forehead. When did we become nurtured by magazines & metal chambers over cellular torsos & four chambers? We become ravens without our stones without our logic. If a body in the desert does not meet water—we want to tell ourselves analogies; believe a violent language does not inhabit our tongues, a violent wall does not murder our neighbors, a violent system does not shoot our people: if we lock ourselves in a room with one table, on one side a pistol & the other a human heart—we want to tell ourselves equations, break us down to numeric, break us down to choice, break us down to no choice, break us down to no voice, break us down. Break us down. Break us down to given ins, give ups, unable to give: whispers seen in light that passes through smoke from barrel to muzzle. Science tells us copper lines our tissues & zinc lines our cells; ancestors remind us, we are not bullets; we are ravens organizing the world; ravens who freeze the sun; messengers. A congress of ravens with power to do, to undo.

Church Ladies Call
about a Christmas Gift

No, not a Barbie, Felicia,
her head shakes & lips purse
receiver in press to her chest,
too expensive. She means
something other. Cheaper;
a thing the church ladies
afford to invest in
something dainty, blonde
anything. Something light
on the pocketbook,
something worthy to give
a kid like me. Something almost
broken, almost breathing.

Dear Coyote

Do you believe in inheritance? The way the abdomen stores the appendix until moment of rupture, until sever. All these vestiges dormant, in wait of cells or motion or the snap of fingers to stir. Coyote, your mangled tales roam the ridges & horizons stinging my vision in what I want to believe is a lament of never homing. I want to believe you never eat fox, you never rip open a throat of a rabbit to taste the jugular, you never swallow a serpent's spine, because you can. I want to believe you follow stars, get lost in their flicker, lick your paws when my belly aches, howl in canyons when my nose bleeds, contort your frame around boulders the shape of my body with ghosts of our ancestors hidden in your muzzle. Your muzzle a cave that spreads under the desert with no sinkhole, no point of entry. I want to say that my shovel pocks the dust & gravel & sedimentary rocks in search of any relic of you. We both unhinge jaws for empty echoes; we both know what it means to haunt.

Lunch Money

Teal-gray punch cards
labeled weekdays
laid out circular dots
at her sneakered feet;
her eyes slivered, *I know
you'll be here. This line
you're accustomed to.* Lines
outside food bank curb
hardest concrete on main
strip of no-stoplight town.
Mom in tears & your belly
only six & ashamed
of its own growls.

Broken Sconce

Circled in filigree, carved out to let light seep in & out of your belly, your plastic bones; a circle yourself; how we're all born rounded—femoral head, apex of heart, capillaries of tissue, thalamus, skull—if only in sections, seen only when dissected down. Your name, *sconce*, requires tongue & teeth & palate to conjure an entire snake from jaws. Etymology in old French *esconse* then Latin feminine past participle *abscondere* to conceal; etymology in a breach of etiquette—a fine imposed; etymology in fortification, & head & wit; we've slung back infinity's trace; how we're all born grounded—to earth or language or chemical be—to ruptured rules & words & shelter. Someone molded your worth separate from being, called you into question; someone discarded you, dripped paint on your skeleton the color of burnt ocher; how we're born into colors & spectrums for all to witness. Not all who witness evoke the lovely; & he found you; he kept you. He kept you among treasures: stuffed parakeet, miniature replica of 1931 Pierce-Arrow, a chirping gold ornament sans Xmas tree; all his treasures lining dusty shelves; treasures of abandonment in his space; he kept you nearer to him than breath, a child's breath; nearer than blood, a whole child's body full; nearer than alchemy, the spell cast to disappear.

Visits

We need to talk to him
Ms. Zamora, how marriage
never belongs to some.
The officer glances, eyes
on my mother, on me
lowers hand from holster.
Substantial damage, he repeats
as if we do not understand
a shattering
of bus windows & words
a Mexican vandal in count
of the only house, of siblings
one, two, three. One, two, three.

Dear Coyote

He spoke a word & in the smooth curves of the S & P & C I wanted
your elbows & shins & the small of your back to materialize, tawny, scent
of cedar chests & hickory chips in every groove, to stand beside me in
scope of language, shield me from a word in claw; he spoke the word
bound by one letter: I. & I knew he spoke beyond you, of us, your seed
that which you carried in your mandible against the scorch of white noise
& white light that gagged you, made you move faster, stealthier, made
you become denser—& you despised the weight, you dropped, grain-
bag of mouth, on the first Desert Dandelion to erect herself for your gait
your lumber. I wanted to believe you wanted to stay; I wanted to believe
even his wicked language might conjure you, reunite us in my eardrums
& we could both be abominations together, making a returnable home
in my body. I know, though, I am a lone thistle in the torrent of letters;
growth to weed out, to drive spade deep in the earth, so no roots remain.

Weight of Indentation

Prayer to Consciousness

Egg yolk on slate; how the child smears
her finger in gelatinous yellow believes
she knows how to contort the sun
around a pinky the size of the universe
heaves solar systems like tetherballs
& we all wonder which snaps first:
the sun or the finger drawing?
How we cord: cells constructed
with adhesion inside: we look
to our navels for signs of life, we look
to our umbilical-causeways, our natural
wombmaps to navigate the space of us
inside our gray matter, the neurons
gather & transmit & speak ill of us
when our cognitive backs turn;
how our brains consist of 60% fat
yet none of this feels cushy or cozy
or delicately open: we question ourselves:
so the yolk, who broke the shell, who
exposes us to all this light in sear, in tear?

Where We Call to Nest

In the brittle scrape of branch upon the pane,
in lift for crack of breeze, a sparrow flies
straight into my chest & mistakes my ribs
for eaves. Her nesting instinct draws her
to the wake of empty, potential for a new
occupant, new residency. She begins to stake
her claim. In peck, my lungs, my liver, my arteries,
my tissues winnow through a pointy warbler's
beak to cast my impure gait, my impure blood,
my impure tongue, my impure cerebrum
to hungry wind. After shuck & caw, light
slats between each vertebra, bone illuminate
to meteorite particles of dust, as some day
returns to dust. After shuck & caw, the sparrow
makes room for twigs & fibers & slivers of metal
& scraps of nylon, a hairpin, bits of plastic:
a collection to furnish, to decorate after the strip
& bare; rawness of me. She makes her plans
with thoughts of hatching: tiny beaks in me. She makes
her plans in renovation, in upheaval, in a faith
of her return to what she has sown. When she shutters
& expands wings for flight, she leaves a frail, *thump,*
thump, thump—heart in suspension—tether of sinew,
tether of shadow, a cavity left unattended, in expose
how papery this organ; how the sun dries cells, salts
down muscles to sand & sea song; how I become
a vessel constructed from other vessels; how my
interments miss the mark, circulate, & deceive
me in thinking, *return* remains possible, absent of belief.

Caught

The belly of the forest exhales—all the wrens & doves & robins & dunnocks & thrushes gather as one singular wing to beat in torrent across the pastures, against the scaffolds of this barn. These birds in stun, their bodies frozen in dizzying flap, mourn relinquish of their unguarded flights & begin to weep; a story, not unlike your story, wedges in their gullets, a lodestone they cannot swallow; their tears release in surge of air to pelt panes, shingles, edges of stone where walls meet the earth. You brought this with you in tuck of flesh, in arc of finger bone, behind the eardrum; wind huffs below the slatted planks of flooring, in the knot holes whistling; ocean of sky upon which your fragile vessel of organs floats; how buoyant must you be now? Polarity a fickle want & aridity unclothes us, bares us nude to the elements, raw & lustful to be carried home in any sort of measure. & in the rattle of saucers, you remember the space between her palm & your cheek, the millimeters in count on your lips now; how calm then rapid, then sting, then regret; the butter dish's tink & clap, parade for the lonesome, summons you into the night; we all more astute in weather—that in which we cannot control; how wings, wings now; how a gale so violent caresses you, catches you on your haunches, burying your wounded lungs into the wounded storm.

& In the Body Keeping

How do we empty
anything from memory?
An imprint depends on flesh
on tremors of electrical impulses,
depends on nervous—how idea
of *system* leaks in & out of
pores—& weight of indentation.
& if a blade? We lacerate:
sculptor becomes the sculpture.
How we carve mutates us. We splay
palms of etches we lick
to taste our identity, our hemoglobin;
we lick to record the taste; we lick
the wound of us: nation
of forgetting, nation of omission.
Where of the keeping? & mind
already in relay of *here, inside, here.*
How in the temporal lobe, we
all limbic murmurs, all hippocampi,
all mammillary bodies, O organs
bound to other organs, let us
memory out of other. Let us
praise the wholeness of cells
the humanity of the amygdala
the veins inside these limbs &
the ability to sculpt & to cut away.
Where keeping manifests biologically
how fingers recall the thread

into the eye; the artist stitches
with rhythm embedded in bone.
The needle all part of the process
burrows a hole, to patch to mend
through sheens of muscle, the body
inscribes this type of keeping, let us
whisper *history* to our forearms
& watch hairs rise in comprehension.

America, Let Us Pause

Because a narrative exists. Let's speak un-hushed & refuse
to collapse from the malicious art of being-taken-away-from.

Speak *scaffolding* & tap your breastbone to acknowledge
the heart of energy, windpipe of power. Power of seeing

mortar & nails exposed—reconfigure beyond a dream, think
American & question every utter of *bootstrap* holding you back;

reconfigure for necessity. Because the absurdity of boundaries.
How we must unlearn rules, draw a map that starts in fluid

of your lungs, burgeons out of flesh, & floods the world
in borderless waves. Because we must love our permeability.

Because a trillion pores in; a trillion pours out. Because land
knows no penciled lines, no round depiction of its existence

in spin under third grader's forefingers. Because third graders'
forefingers. Because kids killed in schools are our fault. Because

awe in the limitlessness: a spectrum of color, ability, queerness,
gender to weave a humanity in refusal of replication. Because

awe. Because love is love. Because Black Lives Matter. Because
guns are humanity's responsibility. Because a president should be

for all people. Because poverty is all our concern. Because her body
is her body. Because disability is not invisibility. Because we label

our failing words; *hate*, our sickness, lodges in our ventricles,
in throats, in our systems, we twist in the weight of the broken

laws who protect the few who wrote the narrative, perpetuate
the narrative, keep the narrative impossible for brown & black &

queer & disabled bodies to step inside. We are sick, country, sick.
Because these words are inadequate. Because poetry requires & yet

cannot encompass. Because we must gather voice. Because a tired soul
is only one yet many souls hold galaxies' weight. Because weight. Because

words *might*. Because voice. Because voice. Because voice. Voice.

Veins & Ghosts & Other Circulatory Systems

Storms: the way a tornado wears a farmhouse inside out; we call this intimacy. We call anything shredded & torn down to the nub, sawdust on our lips: *paradise*. All this motion & emotion, the singularity of the *e* teases your pupils to brain into tinkering inside themselves; clever little collector, the one Time licked & slobbered, shaft in one hand, balls in the other. Still the Sonoran sun melts you down to underarm stench, flushed chest, vaginal lips stuck together; we're papery thin, if we choose to be. *Labia; labia; labia.* The ruggedness between your legs folded just so. How we are whispers in hushed throats, masturbating behind the clothesline pole, desperately wanting the neighbor down the lane to splay fingers & see the sweat on our brow. Isn't all breath, hot breath? This respiratory engine we lug in bone. How can anyone calefaction you like you do? You're a patchwork of tubes; route for oxygen-depleted blood; a four-chambered organ's muse; *ba-bump, ba-bump, ba-bump, ba-*; you're the skip & ghost of skip. Specialist reports your jaws entomb scars & wounds. Teeth a scorn, a lash to buccal mucosa. & of the tongue, esophagus, what damages ensue? We think we control language. *Gullet; gullet; gullet.* Sling a word out far enough, edges boomerang back to you; knock you on the head; make you bleed.

The Exercise of Forgiving

Six months ago, the measuring of whiskey
left in the jug, urine on the mattress, couch
cushions, the crotch of pants in wear. You watch
how breath lifts a chest, how a person breathes—
sick hobbies of when we must. You watch
how you become illiterate at counting.
Six or seven broken breathalyzers; a joke
formulates in your throat & you
choke back your windpipe as punchline.
How many sobs in parking lots before sun
lugged above horizon? The heart hammers
all too familiar songs behind your ribs
& these notes cut away at you. You read online
how television, internet, starving children
in numbers greater than three, polar bears,
rain forests, light from an off direction
all desensitize the human brain's ability
to empathize. You wonder how
you chew the word *panic* in your jaws,
let meaning burrow into molars
seep in crevasses between root & bone.
How rot tends to the insides. You wonder
now with the inpatient tags, the cafeteria visits,
the doctors, the psychiatrists, the *when do you
get to come home*s, the hesitation of our bodies
sharing space again, the words *I have not
drank today* & your brain in flinch, how you
excavate organs for what's left, for salvage.

Invisibly, Yours

I search static for a portrait of an eye; for your real eye rolls in socket away from me, absorbs my tissues in half light, thinks it knows me—distastes me—wants to suck my marrow & spit me wet & disoriented into an urn. The stagnancy lies to me; I'm a whole wound built from synaptic lies; scribble my name & before I ask, erasure—how synthetic rubber burns your jaws in chew; my name grits between pulp & dentin & enamel of molars; you forget me before you know how to speak me. Our thrash & flail temperaments where history winnows my vagina, my Mexican veins, my genetic disposition to die earlier *than*; we call these *unnatural causes*: environment of a single-parent upbringing, weight of oppression. How my relation to someone forgetting; chaffs of me, where I lay down in the fodder next to my own guts & organs & muscle memory; to be ingested or at least tasted once, where you find me in float of your belly's acids, etching my lips to the lining of walls.

Six Functions of Bone

I. *Support*

As in the heaps & heft of skin; 20 pounds of flesh you lug along Earth's
surfaces; an organ of nails & hair; epidermis raincoat & six more layers;
dressings; a garment grown from us as us. A clothesline of sorts; holds
up our limp masses of organs, muscles & skin; what you hang your
face on; a scaffold living inside us living; what our tissues drape from;
combinations of collagen for softness—proteins & varied molecules—
& calcium for strength—steel beam of us; how we embody opposites;
our frame embeds in undersides; our hidden Halloween homages.

II. *Movement*

Fulcrums all we, levers & joints; how the puppet & the puppeteer share the same trunk. See the structure pirouette; strings built in. How lovely & mechanical if you deconstruct any silhouette in locomotion. Muscle attaches to bone & bone; internal stacks; our forces transmit—radio of us; all these connection points in which we articulate from; & in contraction we conjure: magician as magic; *voilà voilà*; mandible articulates with skull; & the silent vaudeville roils, tent expands & stage erects for you—you one-person show—splendors fissure in the dark.

III. *Protection*

You know of safety, bone. You know of wounds & a body spills when sliced, leaks when gashed; of all you try so desperately to hold together, to cradle & keep womb-like for the synapses we call memories; you hold memories in the cavities, in the spongy places we hide away in; the places broken, pinned & clamped back together; the gelatinous tendrils where our worlds implode & grow from; how this soft tissue hardens when attacked, beaten, dehumanized & cowers, refuses to cross vestibules of optic nerves to brain; some of us just hold on tight.

IV. *Blood Cells*

At your interior, let us speak of connectivity; let us speak of marrow in friendship; in names of ilium, ischium, scapula, sacrum, clavicle, carpals, talus, ulna; all the names in which you bind; a gathering in your gentle stature. Do you hear yourself being spoken into existence? You bring the red marrow & you bring the party: erythrocytes, leukocytes, platelets; how you live production; how you seethe a minute world bound in a biconcave disc, no nucleus, to transport our oxygen, our carbon; & when I say *our*, I mean yours; your breath into our tissues.

V. *Mineral Homeostasis*

A seismograph of sorts; how you monitor the tremors of our inland climate; weather vane of sternum & ribs attaches to all that pulsates; how a single neuron fires up to 50 times per second & we are all electrical & humming & needing of nourishment. Consider calcium & phosphorus in levels, minerals as equations; what you do for us, dear bone, dear lover of balance & thwarter of mischief, you love; a love bountiful & harsh you release when must; bone to blood; the delicate art of never being a bystander, of never letting this body fend for need.

VI. *Storage*

Hidden in the diaphysis of the long bones, another marrow forms; let us speak of yellow marrow to understand our age, how our body grows from child to adult & transforms even in the deepest hollows; you take triglycerides, esters of glycerol & fatty acids, & huddle them for safe keeping in our axial skeleton; here you generate fat, cartilage & more bone; yellow the color of fat; what does this say of our head & trunk as collectors; even the most minute parts of us, mimic creation over & over until you, dear bone, believe any birth is possible.

Stones of Mend

Sun gorges orange, designs the clouds pink with hues
of purple—*Ardan Lough* on your lips; the sharp bend
leads you to heaps of stones left to complete the mend
of where a wall will be; you've never been so close to
& so far from, Frost. This fiduciary reconciliation
carved in walls, walls you carry inside; a haunting & you
house; how far a body absorbs space, this necessary
gather & release. Geese cackle over another forest,
another lake mirrors sky to land in another symbiotic
relationship; you smell the dank earth in your hair &
wonder how you etch miles in your ribs; how you hold
desert in your belly lining & when you exhale, particles
of dust spill out, blanketing the marsh; shrill coos break
you from you & black wings dance their threaded loops
above; how foreign & familiar pock firmament; here,
you are a shadow of a shadow beneath tangled bows &
brambles—an echo of tongue not yet unfurled.

Announce

Behind the table, a sprig of an ironwood tree
pokes at the intersection of wall & baseboard.
You crawl, belly to worn carpet, inching, camera
in hands. What *containment* means to a cellular
being in knock at womb's arc meant for us
to tumble out of; our rites of passage nestle
in our sponges & collagen—how a framework
spores out of its own tissues. How we germinate
inside out: seeds not unlike cells, a spreading
behind molecules ready to burst through, show
sprouting hairs & dying integuments to the light
to announce: *Have you been waiting? Waiting long?*

At the Tortoise Corral,
Six Months Sober

You lean over the railing, elbows out
as if every piece of you in contemplation
on this moment; these languid ghosts nest
in your temporal lobe. Just outside our pupils,
the Galápagos tortoises shade themselves
in the morning heat; their stony carapaces
in shelter of the delicate internal; how internal
the momentums of our souls. The Galápagos
tortoise's heart beats six times per minute,
laggard only to a hibernating groundhog
at five beats per minute; how the world
conceives velocity in definition to its organs;
how trivial the haunt of elements. A human
heart beats about 60–100 times a minute
& a hummingbird's heart 1,260. You turn
your chest from me & behind ribs I become
more hummingbird than human; & what of
flutter in coalesce with solicitude? The sun
captures your stature & elongates your frame
into the corral; how briefly you hover
weightless, a shadow not meant for keeping
& I am, again, lost in dense & cumbersome
pauses, lost on the tongue with only a verge
to burst out of my shell, peel this skin, *here,*
here, see me see me & to ask you if silence
wears a body thin; if the long gaps in linear
space may resuscitate anything worth
resuscitating? How a body renders

a universe in its organs, a circulatory servitude
relative to movements of fluids; I search
the ocean of you for rhythms, for echoes
behind your stiff jaw, your sternum, your skull;
all the hard portions of you, not ready to assemble
for me; & of my heart: this *thud, thud* this anchor
I confuse for plow, only heavies the waves
& continues to throb of cadences not its own.

Negative Compliment:
Or Contemplations on Racist Rhetoric

You don't see the back of your own words
the ones grazing my face, the almost hum
in summon on your tongue, to dig a hole
& place me in, just so my brown body makes
sense to you, to lower in your vision, your scoop
as to think my bones for collection, for descent
as in a placement that you control. I shut my eyes,
rest my hand gently upon your shoulder, even
to my own shoulder; I've come to let you: let go
of the tick in the back of your throat, the murmur
of your fragility, of what makes you scared of what
I will take away. Open your eyes: see me: brown
& powerful & releasing this weight you left here
upon my brain, my capillaries, my nervous system.
These are yours. Take your words & let them burn
to ash, so the flame of them cinders the message &
stings your taste buds, so you inhale your own grit,
your own sour smell in your lungs, so your words may
become phoenixes in learn from the scars & sears
they inflicted, become all genders, grow out of each
of your ribs & spread wings of billowing tufts of plume
to release you—out of your own spinal axis—out of
your thoracic trench you continue to dig & dig & dig.

Collective Mend

You are not alone. How a word evolves into an entry point; a phrase too & so too a poem & also, too, a song. Let us consider how to enter *mend*, as vast a universe as any, from page to voice, or voice to page; how to enter heal. *You are not alone.* Let words speak in clarity & remove stigmatic boulders in weight of limbs, of laden organs & desire for safe; let us say *survivor* & believe, believe, believe; let us reframe focus into ethical equations: if a survivor then also a perpetrator. & let these numbers, these 17.7 million reported voices seek mending. Let the *need* to report dissipate. *You are not alone.* Educate, educate, educate, educate until the instinct evokes thoughts only opposite of harm; collective voice we dwell. How fire spreads & sexual violence—an inferno— body of flames, body of society in flames & to turn away from the burn is to burn, to ignore the char inside & the char outside. *You are not alone.* We all one strand of one web, in pluck, in reverberation. We must crumble a dominate narrative; we fight to end the fight's reason— which starts with me & you & you too & you too & you too into loops of human infinity. Violence to one of us *is* violence to all of us.

Universe Wide

Our way, lost, only in breath held—barefoot
in the dusk, our dust-filled organs in sand, wind
erases heel's mark, undoing; lug of a raw body,
shorn by heat of words in inhale, in exhale,
elements held by tongue. How do we speak out
of the dust inside we will become? We return
bone & cells to specks & granules, winnows of
a life—the seed pod scatters, refuses to plant,
the tree already sown—we spread the horizon
across us, memories stretch the universe, wide.

Where the Carriage of My Cells Catch

Headspace Prayer

The cattle dog peers out from the henhouse; protection in all the curious senses. Your silhouette behind an old barn window, both of you wearing your age in the misty afternoon. You both came to be erected here, by determined minds & the hopes of what hands may do; how service & art are somehow sisters. The fly in the lampshade putters sporadically around the bulb, bumping a small body over & over into rounded plastic; the fly in the lampshade resembles rain, & even after the rain begins, you do not know which summoned which. & a prayer lives here, quiet like water pools in sag before droplet; this prayer you do not yet know how to decanter, but you've tasted enough blood & licked enough bodies to know when to take things slow. You think of Limón's sharks & her rivers, your rivers & yet not, & wonder if the fly spun circuitously long enough, would it stop wanting forest? The pasture? The lake? The guts of overgrowth? Across the field, a rooster crows; outside the upper barn, rain ceases, *hallelujah*, & inside as well, *hallelujah*.

Beautiful Fault

Let's say I am significant & this,
how this leads to all possibilities
inside & outside the skull—this too,
a form of logic & fact
of imagination, as imagining itself into
fact—we imagine
ourselves every moment; I
create I; how we find ourselves
in space of each other; how
a page waits
on tiptoes, on edges for
our participation. Do you feel
attention in these inadequate
strokes of language? Foundations
matter. A lack defines only
relative to something other; I am
something other & I love you
regardless of the *without*s
you labeled me, regardless of
your knuckles at my lips &
how I've come to know
the taste of iron in my blood
& I want to believe that makes
me strong. Who gets to decide
what *without* looks like? I ask
but you know that I know;
I know I know—how I find
comfort in questions

you do not wish me to ask
about my body, my brownness
relative to you; relativity
used to be a game
in grammar school, you named
me *greasy spic*, you named me
dirty beaner, my vagina *taco*, you slashed
words at my body, a game
you thought to play me to pock me
to shut me up by gouge
& in the shower, I'd pick
at the holes your words
carved from me, place each
scab on my tongue & spit it out;
each scab torn to deepen the scar—
I wanted to remember
in the mulberry trees
my brother taught me
scars are wounds that bear memories,
gifts of resistance; he squinted
in use of the word *gifts*; what he meant was
it's not my fault
that someone hates me before knowing
I exist; what he meant was
a fault exists in the vault of every universe
& my body is welcome there;
what he meant was
if we fracture a system long enough

our voices build
a neoteric system
with our voices inside;
what he meant was the lived faults
of me gather year over year
& make me whole & love me
& make me whole
& love me; what he meant was
we conceive ourselves first—fact
& tailor the world to hear us,
tailor the world.

Bee in the Barn

Things reflect their intersections.
—TOMMY PICO, *Nature Poem*

I think, at first, another fly, another awkward body in search of
warmth from elements on this country island; I think, this one, too,
may find this space part cave, part echo, part silence shrieking. Then
upon the couch's arm, a bee comes to rest. *What confuses you, bee, here
for sweetness inside these musty walls?* We share the same incandescent
heat of the bulb above, the same wood-burnt-stove linger in the air,
same topography of ceiling in which we tinker with flight; I say
method is the ghost in the mist, because the bee cannot, or would not
with this broken system, this body of dilapidated words; how
language a swarm swelling in the chest, caught in throat; I say *empyrean
is rain in the earthworm*, half expecting the bee to groan & leave; in
my mouth I long to pluck out a molar & another & another &
replace one cavity with a quasar, another with a supernova, &
another hollow with the sun; all this in syzygy, under a canopy of
divided palates; all this flutter: *in the body lives a body of*; a new sky
below folds of hypodermis to guide this bone-map by illumination.

Unlearning

The twisted trees, chest high, multiply in devil's forks
gathering in the lush trenches of ditch; remind you of
the tongue left unattended. Want of maturation &, yet,
inability to tame—to be connected in deep embrace,
the foliage teems & intertwines in such intimacy & orgy
of a natural sort; this lunge & snatch of available space,
a seeking—to root boldly into open air free of meaning
& the hurt inscribed in each syllable, free of worry
weight of language to a body—to crave dusk; how
graying strokes of light wipe across the horizon & how
the elongating shadows caress our curves; to be
imbibed in the bosom of dark, its tales like mother's
murmurs at our earlobes, lulling us; to press palms in
aqueous soil, the cold in greet of our richness of flesh.

On the Legalization
of Concentration Camps in America

I sit, knees to chin, on a brick patio overlooking a small plot
of dirt, not unlike a grave. My father-in-law tells me, *Grass roots
firm. Water it & the grass will return.* Today, *The Nation* reports
the president seeks to unweave the 1997 *Flores* settlement,
take back rules established to protect children, immigrant
children. My eyes burn in blink. I fan my fingers over
the dried soil, over chipped stones & *how our tendings fail*
slips through chapped lips. This is about *who.* 108-degree
heat pummels my flesh & the sweat runs down the back
of my legs & puddles at my seat. *Indefinite detainment* curdles
in my eardrums & my jaws, my jaws remain in a perpetual
state of clench. I come to the sun & stench & sear in search
of *why*: why the word *indefinite* when we should ask ourselves
the *why* behind the act of *detainment*, why three children died
of flu in detention centers this year, why we interchange
child for *inmate*, how our country withholds vaccinations
like water like food like clean air like human decency, how
a brown body means nothing to chins in turn & the *isn't that
just horrible*s & the brains in skulls already planning to cast
their votes to keep the show rolling in the favor of—white
supremacy, the predatory seed in rot of thoughts & actions,
how I long to uncover you, obliterate your spell over
this country; how our minds & language & rules contain
pieces of why. How the dirt haunts, the minute particles
we all return to, haunts me for ways to read the world
to explain my heart in shards, to notify the gasp between
my lungs, the scream living in my trachea of reality after

reality of this nation: where a mother sees kids in body
bags & turns the channel because *they are just immigrants*
& turns the channel because of her whiteness & her kids'
whiteness & how the hierarchy of lives haunts us. I lift
my cheekbones & closed lids directly into the dense
rays of light. *Not a grave. Not a grave. Root firm. Root firm.*

Acts After Addiction

Your stature in the waves; body
a tower made miniscule in the vast
horizon of water. How you peel down
all shoulders; your left collarbone protrudes
above the other; gift of how the bike accident
reconfigured you. How asymmetrical
our amalgamations of anatomical parts; waist-
deep in seaweed you become all gooseflesh,
all impressions of compressions
in sand, washed, swept, as if
erasure finds us a simple act: a flick of tongue
saliva produced, swallowed, made to be
remade—we bring our organs & limbs
& circumventing systems to toe the ocean,
dip our wet insides into the wet outside—
how we long for what makes us. How we
long to taste brine on our papillae. O receptors
in wait for constant stimuli; even our dorsum
divides into symmetrical halves. Born of wet
womb to carry the moist within us into dry
air we must breathe. Our liquid-rendered brains
complicate our memories, our desires
more thirst than any pure impulse. I thirst
inside this limping heart. My chin on my knees,
hugs the shore, pretends not to want to run
after your shadow; to wrestle light means
I must understand horizon hates me just a little
& *at bay, at bay, at bay* lives only in the gray &

brooding gap between cerebellum & throat.
I try to understand your thirst. In truth I am
a piss-poor archeologist & an even worse fortune-
teller. As if *you* were ever mine to keep
masticating between my jaws, on verge of gape
or swallow. Acts of false keeping; how lungs
cannot *keep* the air. Every cell in process
to stave suffocation. How chemically, water
in our cells absorbs shock. Acts of forgetting
muscle memory left after 18 months of seeking
hidden jugs & bottles, of tending to wounds
we both carved out pieces of meat & tissues
littered the floor with remnants, let the dogs
paw them about; even they smelt the sour.
What acts speak of us now? Your brown locks
mesh to your scalp by water's force. I witness
your neck just above the foam; your calm
outline in the agitated tide. You slip
under surf & gently disappear into the roil.

Borderless Wake

No borders speak me, weave me into being; how
language a failed construct, of imaginary lines in limit;
how the word *clavicle* releases from jaws & synapses
from our brains, yet the word *clavicle* fails to be bone, itself,
to never be ridged, raised collagen in grow just below

surface & outside our tongues, our imaginations
let us dwell in land & landscape without arrest. & of borders,
of take & keep, reap & sow: a hand draws over my mouth,
our indigenous mouths, over our immigrant mouths—hand
the smell of wet soil, of iron, the scent of blood.

If you draw a line in the sand, the surf swallows
what you have done; disobedient tide song, demonstrative
& irregular, eager for no one & all. In our conch shell ears,
rules beat in the reef & seashores, the same brine
inside you; how this has always been about

what's inside you. No borders inhabit our biology,
chemically speaking, genetic, born only from parts we label
to understand our own anatomies. Most borders spawn
from our psychological sickness of dominance
of colonization, of war. Do you want to brick

up my skin, mortar my organs, mortar my cells behind
a wall? Encapsulate my blood for if & when you wish
to spill it? Who made you mason & my body masonry?
Hemispheres of our brains imagining world; internal we
comprise of the same gray matter, same borderless wake.

Prayer to the Charcoal Dusk

A shadow rattles inside this suit of cells, in wait for headlights on the horizon. You pray the driver knows you, knows you lay in the center of concrete, a piece of a center line only existing outside double yellows & laws matching intention.

— — —

Face of slivered moon questions you; glow penetrates topical everything, flesh. A miniature finger of a miniature woman swishes tip on the backside of your sternum. She sits cross-legged behind your manubrium on lumps of tissues, feels her way into fibers, takes out her miniature chisel & begins to etch the story of a hummingbird's birth. She carves only vowels & plus signs; miracles of mathematics & the scrape of metal on bone into magic.

— — —

What absorption means funneling through lightless tunnels. We call these passages, pupils. We call these passages, witness. We call these passages up our throats into conjure, mis ojos solo pueden soportar tanto, a prayer in bleed.

— — —

Creases of her knuckles smell of wind flowing south; your lips open 585 miles away amid striations of rock & stone as moisture pools on your tongue in the shape of her name.

— — —

You carry more dusk in your lungs than a billion sunsets burning together. Weight of char, of firearms in schools & children in plead, *don't let them kill us today*, of construction of walls & children in concentration camps on american soil, of the kitchen with blackface figurines next to the stove, of acronyms & ICE raids & the man from your university on trial—hung jury—for giving water to the thirsty in the desert, of *bang bang bang*—someone thought funny to light fireworks off in El Paso days after, of the words *great* & *america* in any proximity to each other, of your aortic sack in wrench of headlines & ticker tapes. You carry more dusk in your lungs than a billion sunsets burning.

– – –

Creases of your knuckles smell of soil just before rain, lowest root to bark of the sycamore. The closest sycamore tree to your nose remains in California & Mexico. You close your eyes to pray the wet from the night; the wet here too.

– – –

Face of three-quarters moon questions you; light penetrates your muscle. A miniature knee of a miniature woman bends to scale your vertebrae. She stables each foot in bone's crevasse before lift & hull of her weight. Her palms bleed. She began in the sacral, traversing her miniature body through lumbar to thoracic. She pauses on the mountain of your spine to wipe fluid & bits of tissues from her eyes. Throws her head back to a cellular sky. Six more juts of bone to go before she reaches the seven cervical. Hums escape her mouth, *aaaa . . . ooooo . . . uuuuu . . . eeeeeaaaaayeeeayeeaeoooooyayaya*; in deep breath she climbs.

— — —

You sit on hot bricks outside your desert home. You imagine us before language, before the tongue flicks the roof of mouth & a lullaby juts out. Our bodies mechanisms for action & the mouth forms from smooth & round edges & muscle & we think *purpose*. The first person to kill another person acted before speech; where did we learn the fever of taking? You imagine false inception. You image the seeds of *honor* from *horror*. You wish the night a cradle inside you; the lullaby that never hatches.

— — —

Creases of your knuckles smell of placenta, branching loops of blood vessels on the baby's head after birth. You do not remember the canal or the forceps or the pungent disinfectant birthing suite or the sting of light. Instead, you remember how the cold compressed your tiny lungs & rippled throughout your rib cage into song.

— — —

Face of full moon questions you; your bone aghast in all illumination. A miniature sack where a miniature heart suspends in a miniature woman, ruptures as her arms & legs & torso crawl toward your cerebellum. Her climb past the cervical vertebra, past the medulla oblongata, leaves her miniature body in spasms & contorts & shakes; your lips stutter in vowels. She creeps in caterpillar form, deep into the gelatinous tissues, a maze where she lays on her back & begins to chunk out pieces of fiber, pieces of gray matter. Before her chest collapses & your organ swallows her miniature frame, she sees the moon; moon round spilling prayers from her cratered face; moon full & disfigured in the missing tufts of brain.

Congruence

My limbs & organs fold in bark, ridged slits
of definition to a worn & weathered frame
surface bares the harsh of dust spit in wind, sun,
eyes in midst of shaming me, elements of wicked
tongues hurling wicked words; where sap weeps
from a trunk: so too a torso in prick & pock—
blood on the outside of flesh, a wound, not a stain
& the bullseye rings around around—dare I say
ring of me, of all this churn & whir, in circulatory
systems that fuel & break my body into bread, blood
into wine, & no one's hungry & no one's thirsty, no
covenant made to honor any part of bone & thorn.
I'd wash the gouge in baptismal anything, if human
utterances made any water purer than the river, stream,
the lake—how dirt grits everything, makes our jaws
aware of our own taste & our cracks more natural
upon our throbbing lips; raised bark, open as if.

Upon Never Meeting My Father

My father holds quartz in his hand, *Whittle it sharp enough, you could cut your Achilles*. He snickers & I watch with wet eyes, closed, humid musk permeates the horizontal of my body laying among dewy corn, knees & wrists & thighs still & silent as— *The dead*, he says, *flip open their eyelids in their coffins to chuck damnation back at the living*. He flicks his fingers into my face quick, quicker, as if he's casting a spell; I do not move, do not flinch. He does not know which of us is *the dead* in this equation. I have no heart to tell him.

He combs my hair with thumbs; he combs my hair with scents of a hundred boxelder bugs just before dawn; he combs my hair with pliers, pulls out mats of hair, follicles like onion bulbs says, *Your grandmother Petra lost her two front teeth at 37*, turns from me & I know his back means we are lineage in pieces. I run my tongue over grooves of a smile, hidden between closed lips.

Below the lip of the forest, he holds my hand, lifts me over the bramble, lets the thorns slice & tear at my ankles & shins. *Blood binds you*, his snort echoes with the sheep grunts & exhaust pipes from the old highway, & he licks his knuckles as if the earth sticks like sinew between his incisors, & I pray to the June bugs in July he doesn't know what he's saying, doesn't understand geometry & magic & a spinal cord in quaver of a cell it never knows a cell in tonal scrape & doesn't know how limbs of a mulberry tree are never meant to hug his daughter's flesh to sleep, how milk & blood sour in all this heat.

This Preparation of All Things Autumnal

I thumb the leaves half in bloom
in cling to branches—no one
tells us: let, let, let—& go looms
inside our cells. This morphology
of a belly begins corded to another
belly as keeper, as fuel, as trunk
to limb. We carve out first from in.
We carve from in to out.
How we pullulate. Send forth
sprout of us. I guess I am saying
if you crack my femur in half
& analyze the cross section
map of hairline sponges nestled
in a warped circle of compact,
one side is me & the other side
the *dream* of me. & I speak both
of bone. Mouth full of pulp & dentin
& enamel & cementum. I speak
from the vessels lining my jaws
to the ribs stacked, neatly so.
What distance lies between each
rib in jut from my spine? I count
because I know how. I count
because even the atoms inside me
bond together & my mind speaks
without permission, *molecules*
O molecules & these bodies of linger,
patterns from the missing. I gape, not

unlike the trachea. Yet the trachea
consists of tube & what of the hole
when my cerebrum fails to synapse
& the finality of an empty skull
or the tree, barren, in icy field hunkers
into mount of dirt, roots first? I thirst
for the leaf's secret. I long for the *wind*
of windpipe, the reticent change
of pigment & all these biological
agreements, the acceleration of loss
of chlorophyll, this preparation of all
things autumnal, of the shrug before frost.

Ingress

In the lough near twilight, swans gather
in their white gowns—specters lambent
on the glassy lake—pirouette & spy me
spying; our elegant necks cull each other
in dark brume, this palliative obsidian—
pupils of menace—*chatter chatter*—never
ceases, in wisps & wonders of jaws
unhinging, filling with bodies of stars.

Prayer of the Palo Verde Beetle

I watch a Palo Verde beetle on its back, flail tibia spurs & tarsi & antenna next to the gas station pump. Heat of crude oil, of carbon atoms in absorption; heat of desert in August suffocates my thighs & sweat runs course of my legs in frozen witness. I am spiracles pin pricking a body trying to breathe. I am elytra to cement. I carry migration in my scutum: a song unraveling over generation after generation & yet a border weighs on mind & mandible, a bullseye on my back, on the backs of those of us who sing across imaginary lines with inherited wings. Gooseflesh exists before ticker tape, before the shooter, before brown bodies agape & words consume & images consume & we look to the sky for semblance of song & a wall becomes a scalpel in rip across abdomen of continent which first born an entrance, a womb. I am compound eye meeting brown irises in firmament. I am cloud-cover prayer. Foot in reach to turn over & I collapse in a nation's hesitation. I am pupils in drill, aghast.

Dear Coyote

I tire of this nation. A nation in gash at the seams. A nation divvying out razorblades, eyes narrowing on us. A nation that locks our brown children in cages. A photo of a father & daughter facedown in river water. My stomach lurches. Head dizzies & pounds. I burn under flesh. A nation that uses words of *detention* & *custody* to barter lives for a wall. From its belly we chant *concentration camps. Stop! Stop!* We cannot suture wounds the nation gnashes teeth in, bites chunks from, & plots to make a graveyard of our bones still inside our walking flesh. I tire of this nation. I long to haunt back. I incorrectly speak of heaven as a place where all bodies may inhabit. I tug each of my hairs from follicle, cord end to end & weave a net; kiss my fibrous compositions & toss them into wind, into atmosphere, into the fueling dark of space where the carriage of my cells catches a nebula. Some refer to nebulae as *star nurseries*, regions where new stars begin to form. Our safe dwelling. I pull us up from earth, into ether.

Game Sanctuary

> Every one of us with a bear inside.
> —ADA LIMÓN, *Sharks in the Rivers*

Rusted metal leans—redefines
crooked. This canopy of forgotten.
How you cock your head
to become the structure. Barbed
wire laces this crop of land, a limb
of thorns reaches into a plum horizon—
all things never meant for picking.
How our vision tethers us
in keeping; we hold & lengthen
to pupil's absorption; you ask me
to speak of ghosts, beneath the mist;
we laugh from our hollow bones. Wet
& emerald leaves on our cheeks
in eve of December, firelight melts
our bodies raw & burns cold
the tips our fingers & we remember
in chests to breathe, to see our whispers
condense on panes, how in pastures
sheep's wool spray-painted red & green
for season & the mouth of inlet opens
to the throat of the lake—a still
that's never still: my heart fumbles,
behind these fences, beyond the guttural
sirens of distant cattle, I lay agape
my pulmonary trunk in expose
of vessels & heat on cobble stones
gulping: an offering of what may be.

In Gratitude

AN ENORMOUS THANK YOU to the entire team at the University of Iowa Press, and James McCoy for guiding this process and making the birth of this book possible. Magicians, all of you.

Mountains of gratitude to Brenda Shaughnessy for selecting my book to win the Iowa Poetry Prize. It's surreal to have a poet whom I admire so deeply call my art forward. Gracias. Gracias. Gracias for giving this book a place in the conversation of poetry.

Much love to Diana Marie Delgado, Jos Charles, and Danez Smith for their poetry which inspires me, and their generous words on my art—mil gracias. Many thanks to Silvia Andrade for use of this stunning artwork to make this cover come alive.

I am truly honored by the people who take a chance on my art and help it live in the world. Thank you to the editors and editorial teams from the following magazines, journals, and presses in which these poems first appeared: Academy of American Poets, Poem-a-Day ("The Exercise of Forgiving"), *The American Poetry Review* ("Beautiful Fault"), *Atlanta Review* ("Where We Call to Nest"), *Boston Review* ("For Survival of Migration: Or That Which They Cannot Devour," "Motel," "Dear Coyote" [page 15]), *Crazyhorse* ("Bee in the Barn"), *The Georgia Review* ("This Preparation of All Things Autumnal"), *Hunger Mountain* ("Dear Coyote" [page 8] and "Dear Coyote" [page 18]), *Hayden's Ferry Review* ("Homing Anatomy"), *jubilat* ("Closer"), *The Laurel Review* ("Six

Functions of Bone," "Veins & Ghosts & Other Circulatory Systems"), *Lumina* ("Game Sanctuary," "Prayer to Consciousness"), *Missouri Review* ("Headspace Prayer"); *The Nation* ("Bodies & Water"), *New Limestone Review* ("& In the Body Keeping"), *Orion* ("Prayer of the Palo Verde Beetle"), *Permafrost* ("Broken Sconce," "Memory of Sheep Rustling"), *Prairie Schooner* ("Negative Compliment: Or Contemplations on Racist Rhetoric"), *Puerto del Sol* ("Upon Never Meeting My Father"), *Sonora Review* ("Devil's Tongue"), *Sycamore Review* ("Prayer to the Charcoal Dusk"), *The Volta* ("Invisibly, Yours").

Thank you to Rebecca O'Connor and Will Govan, cofounders and editors of *The Moth* and hosts of The Moth Retreat for Artists and Writers in Ireland. Sections of this manuscript would not have existed without their tremendous space that welcomes and rejuvenates artists. Your residency helped me remember that I cannot escape the inner droning voice, nor do I want to.

Huge hugs and thanks to M McDonough for gifting me with their words for the title of this manuscript. They generously blessed the union of my manuscript and their words—and that's how magic happens. Heart you.

To my CantoMundo family, you came into my life at a time when I needed community more than ever. Some of these poems only existed in your chest first. The abrazos and laughs and tears connected me, and this art, in deep and necessary ways. You made me palpable in my own skin—visible, seen. I open my arms wide for each of you. Loves.

To my family, friends, and communities, your support and belief in me as a human make the venture into this poetic existence possible. Mel, Joe, Mom—the gratitude rolls into infinity.

To Chris, I'd unravel without you. You know this, because you know me. Thank the holy universe you do.

IOWA POETRY PRIZE AND
EDWIN FORD PIPER POETRY AWARD WINNERS

1987 Elton Glaser, *Tropical Depressions*
   Michael Pettit, *Cardinal Points*

1988 Bill Knott, *Outremer*
   Mary Ruefle, *The Adamant*

1989 Conrad Hilberry, *Sorting the Smoke*
   Terese Svoboda, *Laughing Africa*

1990 Philip Dacey, *Night Shift at the Crucifix Factory*
   Lynda Hull, *Star Ledger*

1991 Greg Pape, *Sunflower Facing the Sun*
   Walter Pavlich, *Running near the End of the World*

1992 Lola Haskins, *Hunger*
   Katherine Soniat, *A Shared Life*

1993 Tom Andrews, *The Hemophiliac's Motorcycle*
   Michael Heffernan, *Love's Answer*
   John Wood, *In Primary Light*

1994 James McKean, *Tree of Heaven*
   Bin Ramke, *Massacre of the Innocents*
   Ed Roberson, *Voices Cast Out to Talk Us In*

1995 Ralph Burns, *Swamp Candles*
   Maureen Seaton, *Furious Cooking*

1996 Pamela Alexander, *Inland*
   Gary Gildner, *The Bunker in the Parsley Fields*
   John Wood, *The Gates of the Elect Kingdom*

1997 Brendan Galvin, *Hotel Malabar*
   Leslie Ullman, *Slow Work through Sand*

1998 Kathleen Peirce, *The Oval Hour*
   Bin Ramke, *Wake*
   Cole Swensen, *Try*